Cloze Reading

READING LEVEL 4

REM 414

AUTHOR: **Marth C. Reith**

A TEACHING RESOURCE FROM

REMEDIA
PUBLICATIONS

www.rempub.com

REMEDIA PUBLICATIONS, INC.
SCOTTSDALE, AZ

BLACKLINE
MASTERS

INTRODUCTION

The cloze procedure is incorporated into this unit as a springboard for comprehension. When students complete a cloze passage and have the opportunity to discuss their responses, more significant growth in the comprehension takes place. The students not only gain a greater understanding of concepts, but they expand their vocabulary, as well. This unit uses the cloze procedure for comprehension and it includes a series of questions for discussion of each selection. This added feature insures that the student has a broad understanding of the story by incorporating thinking skills as well as recall activities. The questions involve inference, prediction, and relationship.

The words in this passage have not been deleted at random. Care was taken to include all of the parts of speech and an effort was made to avoid deletions that would confuse the student. For deletions within each passage, answers are selected from the words in the box. This procedure eliminates the frustration that many students encounter because they are more likely to experience success.

The stories featured in this unit have unusual content, which should make them highly interesting to students. The selections are presented in gradually increasing length and difficulty. When students are gradually exposed to more challenging material, their reading skills generally grow.

The cloze format is equally valid for testing. The selections may also be used to assess the student's readability level.

Suggestions: After students complete Cloze Reading, a second reading before answering questions is recommended.

CONTENTS

Name _____

Do Snakes Fly????

is	the	of	holds
say	snake	ground	the

Do snakes fly? In India there _____ a type of snake known as

_____ "flying snake." It can glide through _____

air from a tree to the _____. It flattens out its body and

_____ itself straight. This position lets the _____

"fly" and land in safety. Experts _____ that the snake uses this means

_____ travel only in emergencies.

1.   What is the name of the country where the "flying snake" is found?

_____

2.   How does the snake hold its body when it is "flying"?

_____

3.   When does the "flying snake" use this strange means of travel?

_____

4.   Do snakes really fly? What does this unusual snake do?

_____

_____

5.   Name at least three animals and tell how each animal travels.

_____

_____

_____

Name _____

Deep Freeze

it	climates	standing	because
90	as	temperature	freeze

Strange things happen in very cold _____. In Siberia, a record

temperature of _____ degrees below zero was recorded. At this

_____, ice is like stone. Snow is _____ hard as

table salt. A person _____ outside without the right clothing would

_____ as hard as a rock. However, _____ is

impossible to get a cold _____ the air is too cold for the germs to live.

1.   What was the record low temperature recorded in Siberia?

     _____

2.   What happens to ice? What happens to snow?

     _____

     _____

3.   What would happen to you if you didn't wear the proper clothing?

     _____

     _____

4.   What is the proper clothing for very cold climates?

     _____

     _____

5.   Name a group of people that live in a very cold climate and tell how they dress.

     _____

     _____

The Largest Living Animal

be	throat	living	as
grown	9	is	much

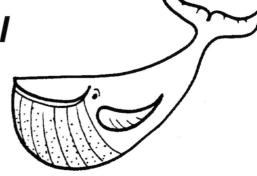

The blue whale is the largest _____ animal in the world. A full-

_____ whale may sometimes grow as long _____

100 feet. It may weigh as _____ as 120 pickup trucks. Even

an elephant _____ small beside a whale. However, the

_____ of the blue whale is only _____ or 10 inches

wide. So, you won't _____ swallowed if you should meet a blue whale!

1. What is the largest living animal in the world?

   _____

2. How much may the whale weigh when it is full-grown?

   _____

3. What animal is small beside a whale?

   _____

4. How wide is the throat of the blue whale?

   _____

5. Why would it be difficult for the blue whale to swallow you?

   _____

6. Name the smallest animal you can think of without naming an insect.

   _____

A Strange Shave

face	tall	man	clean
large	the	as	seed

If you lived in Panama, you would never need to buy a razor. When a Panama

Indian needs a shave, he just goes to the edge of a grassy field. He pulls a thick,

_____ stalk. He removes one of the _____

seeds that grow in bunches on _____ stalk. On the sides of each

_____ are two thin blades as sharp _____ glass.

Holding the seed carefully, the _____ from Panama draws it across his

_____. Off go his whiskers! What a _____ shave!

1. What does the Panama Indian do when he needs a shave?

    _____

2. What does he use instead of a razor?

    _____

3. What might happen if the man is careless when holding the seed?

    _____

4. What does a man do to his face before using his razor?

    _____

5. What are some reasons why the Panama Indian does not use an electric shaver?

    _____

    _____

Name _____

The World's Laziest Animal

even	never	of	for
even	hours	a	sags
it	in		

Don't count on watching a sloth _____ fun! This animal does

nothing for _____ and hours.

The sloth will not _____ flinch at a sudden noise.

If _____ sloth is dropped from a height, _____

will stay in the same position _____ which it lands. Then, it just

_____ like a sack of flour. It _____ bothers to

stand up. Sloths can _____ turn their breathing off for periods

_____ time. Now, that's a lazy animal!

1. What is the name of the world's laziest animal?

    _____

2. What happens when the sloth is dropped from a height?

    _____

3. Find two things in the story that show how lazy the sloth is.

    _____

    _____

4. Name at least one animal that is very active—just the opposite of the lazy sloth.

    _____

Name _____

Doggy Diets

puppies	dogs	progress	up
problems	your	dog	sure
fresh	back		

Dog doctors say that we feed our _____ too much food. They

have come _____ with a diet program for dogs.

　　If _____dog is overweight, you should:

• Make _____ your dog has lots of exercise.

• Cut _____ on your dog's food a little at a time.

• Always have _____ water for your dog.

• Weigh your _____ once a week to see his

_____.

　　The doctors warn that over-feeding _____ and older dogs may

lead to _____ that will shorten your dog's life.

1.　What do dog doctors say we do to our dogs?

　　_____

2.　How many times a week should you weigh your dog?

　　_____

3.　What should you always have available for your dog? _____

4.　Do you have a dog? Is your dog overweight? What do you feed your dog?

　　_____

　　_____

Rowing Across the Ocean

began	Frank	food	to
a	believed	the	build
would	stove	could	had
would	Sometimes		

Do you believe that a person could cross the ocean in a rowboat? Many years ago,

two men did just that. Their names were George Harbo and _____

Samuelson. Both men were sailors. They _____ they could row from

New York _____ France. They both worked hard to

_____ a boat. They thought if they _____

row 54 miles a day, it _____ take them two months to cross

_____ ocean. They had fresh water, a _____, and

food on their boat. They _____ many problems but they were lucky.

_____ big ships would see them. They _____

go on board the ships for _____ hot meal and get fresh water

and _____ to store in their boat. Two months from the time they

_____ their trip, they stepped on shore in France.

1.   What did George Harbo and Frank Samuelson want to do?

_____

2.   Did they have experience on the ocean? How do you know?

_____

3.   Where did they start? Where were they going?

_____

Name _____

Thriller

end	not	to	really
hair	grinning	eyes	has
muscles	on	angry	behind
of	only		

It is possible for your hair_____ stand on end if you are

_____ scared. Each hair root on your head _____

a muscle that can pull your _____ straight up. Even cats have these

_____. When a cat is frightened or _____, the

hair on its back stands _____ end. The human hair muscles have

_____ been used very much, so they work _____

in verry, very unusual cases _____ fright. Look out! There's a zombie

_____ you! His face is torn and his _____ are staring

straight ahead. He is _____ at you.

Is your hair on _____ ?

1.   What can happen to your hair if you are very frightened?

      _____

2.   What is on each hair root that can pull your hair straight up?

      _____

3.   What animal is mentioned in the story as an example of this strange situation?

      _____

4.   What else might happen to human hair if a person is badly frightened?

      _____

Name _____

Helicopters, Whirlybirds, Egg Beaters, Choppers

due	in	Almost	like
could	be	use	France
people	they	100	owe
used	that	War	

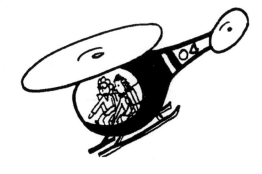

Helicopters have come a long way. _____ 200 years ago, a man

in _____ saw a Chinese toy top that looked _____

what we know as a helicopter. He thought he _____ make the toy large

enough for _____ to fly. He made models, but _____

never flew. It took nearly another _____ years before anyone made a

helicopter _____ left the ground.

Finally, during World _____ II, helicopters flew well enough to

_____ used. Many rescues at sea were _____ to the

"whirlybirds." Helicopters, sometimes called "choppers," were _____

very often during the Vietnam War. Hospitals _____ them today to

airlift patients. Many people _____ their lives to the "egg beater"

_____ the sky.

1.   Write as many names as you can think of for *helicopter.*

    _____

    _____

2.   What kind of toy made nearly 200 years ago looked like a helicopter?

    _____

Good Luck Spots

tell	on	signs	to
causes	nail	luck	being
the	near	or	of
makes	grows	these	

Have you ever had white spots _____ your fingernails?

Do you know what _____ them? Some people call them "good

_____ spots." They are really little bits _____ nail

that are not perfect. The _____ is made of living cells. Sometimes

_____ cells in the nail just don't _____ a perfect

nail. As the nail _____, these spots are pushed out. Sometimes

_____ white marks come from a cut _____ a

bruise. Sometimes the injury is _____ the line where the nail is

_____ formed. Of course, it doesn't hurt _____

think of these white spots as _____ of good luck. You can never

_____!

1. What causes white spots on the nails?

    _____

2. What do some people call these white spots?

    _____

3. What is a nail made of?

    _____

Name _____

Wanted: Dead or Alive

garbage	seen	"wanted"	from
or	cattle	the	what
of	They	their	reward
Jesse	up	toads	

Can you imagine people putting up _____ posters for

toads? This is just _____ happened in Australia. A special kind

_____ toad, the BUFO MARINUS, was brought _____

South America to help the Australians. _____ had too many cane

beetles. The _____ were good at eating these beetles. That's

not all they ate! When _____ beetles were gone, the toads ate

_____, ping pong balls, dogs, cats, and _____.

They killed the animals first with _____ poison. The Wildlife

Department offered a $30.00 _____ for each toad brought in, dead

_____ alive. The "wanted" posters were put _____

all over the country. Imagine what _____ James would have said if he

had _____ his poster next to the picture of a toad?

1.   "Wanted" posters were put up for toads in what country?

_____

2.   The toads were brought in from what continent?

_____

3.   Name two things the toads ate besides the beetles.

_____

Name _____

The Saltiest Lake

a	the	difficult	It
water	hard	the	covered
of	in	to	the
is	really	is	rocks

Imagine floating on your back in _____ water for hours at a time.

_____ is possible to do this in _____ world's saltiest

lake. The Dead Sea, the unusual name for the lake, _____ so full

of chemicals it is _____ hard for anyone to drown. The chemicals

work to keep your body floating. The _____ is so heavy, it is also

_____ to swim. Each stroke you take _____

like pushing away a load of _____. It's so easy to float in

_____ Dead Sea that people do funny things. It is really a crazy sight

_____ see someone lying there, on top of the water, holding an umbrella

in one hand and _____ book in the other. That is what is called reading

_____ comfort. There is only one thing wrong with that. When you get

out _____ the water, your back will be _____ with an

oily film that is _____ to get off.

1. What is the name of the world's saltiest lake?

   _____

2. What happens to you when you get out of the water?

   _____

   _____

Name _____

Miss Piggy Would Hate This

the	*Pigs*	Miss	out
in	of	I'll	instrument
Kermit	pigtail	instrument	pig
were	pitch	tails	worked
To	the		

You've heard of *The Three Little* _____, Porky Pig, and

Miss Piggy, but _____ bet you've never heard a concert

_____ pigs. Over a hundred years ago, _____

1851, a very unusual _____ was shown in England. It was called the

_____ organ. The person who invented this _____

collected a herd of swine. Each _____ had a squeal of a different

_____. The tails of these musical pigs _____

attached to pincers. (These pincers pinched the _____ of

the pigs.) The pincers were _____ by the keys of the organ.

_____ play the instrument, the player pressed _____

keys he wanted. The pigs squealed _____ a melody. The people loved

it! _____ Piggy, if you don't behave yourself, _____

might just rent you out to _____ inventor of the pigtail organ.

1.   What was the name of the unusual musical instrument in this story?

_____

13 *Cloze Reading (Level 4)*

Name _____

Did Columbus Eat Ice Cream?

say	a	Maryland	ice
even	she	an	of
House	cream	ice	400
book	a	same	that	ball

Ice cream was not invented by one person at one special time. We don't know exactly

when people began eating ice cream.

Many people believe that _____ cream did come from Italy. Some

_____ that Italians were eating ice cream _____

before the discovery of America.

When _____ Italian noblewoman became Queen of France,

_____ took her tools for making ice _____ with

her. So, they were eating _____ cream in Paris, too, more than

_____ years ago. In the year 1769, a _____

printed in London, England, had _____ recipe for ice cream. About

that _____ time, there is a record of a lady serving ice cream at

a _____ in New York. We also know _____

Dolly Madison, the wife of President Madison, served ice cream in the White

_____ .

The first factory for the making _____ ice cream began in 1851 in

_____ . Ice cream has been around for _____ long

time. Maybe Columbus did eat ice cream.

Did Columbus Eat Ice Cream?

1. Where do many people believe ice cream came from?

   _____

2. When was a recipe for ice cream printed?

   _____

3. Where was ice cream served in New York?

   _____

4. Who was Dolly Madison?

   _____

5. When was ice cream first made in a factory?

   _____

6. Do we know exactly who invented ice cream and when it was invented?

   _____

7. In what state was the first ice cream factory?

   _____

8. What flavor of ice cream do you like?

   _____

Name _____

The Great Escape Artist

famous	who	course	handcuffs
in	put	helper's	around
for	was	pairs	Then
with	in	all made	was

Houdini was the greatest escape artist _____ ever lived. He could

escape from _____, ropes, straitjackets, or leg irons.

Of _____, his escapes were not really magic. He did have

a helper, though, that _____ his tricks look like magic. His

_____ name was Jim Collins.

Jim worked _____ Houdini for almost 20 years. He

_____ a great mechanic. He could build _____ kinds

of trick locks.

The most _____ escape that Houdini did took place

_____ a river. The river was covered _____ ice

except for one hole. Five _____ of handcuffs were locked on Houdini.

_____ he was put into a box. The cover _____

nailed shut. Finally, ropes were put _____ the box. The box was then

_____ in the river through the hole _____ the ice.

Houdini got out in three minutes. Jim Collins was the man who helped Houdini make

this great escape. He put all the keys into the box while all eyes were on Houdini!

The Great Escape Artist

1. What was the name of Houdini's helper?

   _____

2. What was Jim Collins besides being Houdini's helper?

   _____

3. Where did Houdini's most famous escape take place?

   _____

4. How many pairs of handcuffs were locked on Houdini?

   _____

5. How did Jim help Houdini make his escape?

   _____

   _____

6. How long did Jim work for Houdini?

   _____

7. Name all the ways that Houdini was tied or locked or covered before his great escape.

   _____

   _____

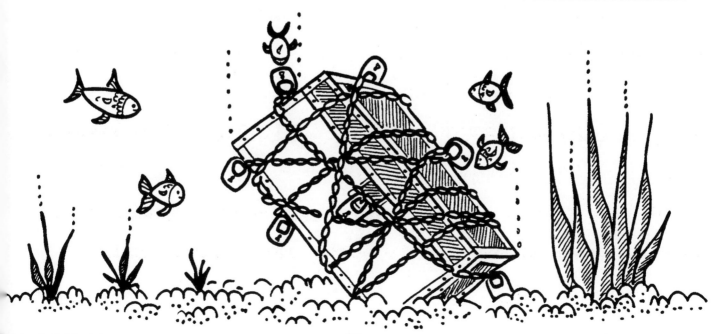

Name _____

Close Encounters

from	time	were	last
visiting	seen	One	getting
businessman	in	state	of
planes	caught	nine	that
soon	seemed	phoned	to

Some people believe that aliens are _____ the earth. Some say

they have _____ flying saucers! What do you think?

_____ summer almost 40 years ago, a _____

was flying his plane across the _____ of Washington. A flash of light

_____ his eye. He turned and saw _____ bright

objects flying very fast. They _____ to be shaped like saucers. He

_____ the newspaper with his story as _____ as he

landed.

A year after _____, a huge flying object was seen

_____ the sky over Kentucky. It seemed _____ be

headed for Goodman Air Base. Three _____ were sent after it. One

_____ the pilots said the object was _____ away

from him. Those were his _____ words. Later, pieces of his plane

_____ found in the area.

Since that _____, there have been hundreds of reports of UFO's

(Unidentified Flying Objects) _____ all over the world.

Close Encounters

1. What did the businessman see while flying his plane?

   _____

2. What did the businessman do when he landed?

   _____

   _____

3. How many planes were sent after the UFO near Goodman Air Base?

   _____

4. What do you think happened to the pilot who said it was getting away from him?

   _____

   _____

   _____

   _____

5. What do the letters "UFO" stand for?

   _____

6. Do you believe flying saucers or UFO's exist? Why or why not?

   _____

   _____

   _____

Name _____

Vampires Live

movie	These	America	when
you	250	of	the
carry	picks	Sometimes	off
nests	at	their	birds
to	the	their	

Vampires do exist! No, not the _____ kind of vampire, but vampire

bats! _____ bats are one type of over _____

kinds of bats. They live in _____ tropics and actually suck the blood

_____ their victims. They do not usually go after humans. They

have been known to _____ rabies, a deadly disease, from animal

_____ animal.

Bats are animals and not _____. The mother bats have milk in

_____ breasts for the young bats. Usually _____

female gives birth to one baby _____ a time.

Bats do not make _____ for their young. When the bats go

_____ at night, the young bats go with the mothers. They ride

hanging onto _____ mothers' necks. _____ the

mother will leave her baby on a branch of a tree. It hangs, covered by leaves. She

_____ it up when she returns.

Luckily, _____ don't have to cover your neck

_____ you see a bat in North _____. If you go to the

tropics, though, watch out!

Vampires Live

1. Where do the vampire bats live?

   _____

2. What do the bats do to their victims?

   _____

   _____

3. What disease do these bats sometimes carry?

   _____

4. What do the bats do with their young when they go off to look for food?

   _____

   _____

5. Bats are not birds. What are they?

   _____

6. What kind of vampires exist?

   _____

7. When do the bats fly?

   _____

8. How many kinds of bats are there?

   _____

Ghost Towns

11,000	towns	there	ran
on	sprang	and	famous
was	great	Virginia	1859
People	furniture		

Do you believe ghost towns are _____ where ghosts live? Of course not! We have many ghost towns in America. No one knows how many

_____ are. Whenever men discovered riches in oil, lumber, silver, or

gold, towns _____ up. They quickly died out _____

became ghost towns once the riches _____ out.

One of the most _____ ghost towns is Virginia City,

Nevada. The _____ Comstock silver lode was discovered in

_____.

At that time, Virginia City had _____ people. The U.S. mint set

up an office there to make silver dollars. _____ built beautiful homes.

They bought fine _____. Mark Twain, the famous author, worked

_____ the newspaper there.

What happened to _____ City? The silver ran out. Nothing

_____ left to keep the people there. Grass and tumbleweeds now cover

the streets. Only the ghosts of the past remain in the ruins of the once fine homes.

22

Ghost Towns

1. What are ghost towns?

   _____

   _____

2. How did some towns become ghost towns?

   _____

   _____

3. What is the name of one of the most famous ghost towns in Nevada?

   _____

4. What was mined in this area?

   _____

   _____

5. What happened to Virginia City after the riches ran out?

   _____

6. What famous author worked on the newspaper in Virginia City?

   _____

A Great Showman

something	circus	him	Barnum
America	New	advertising	did
He	fortune	play	music
people	get		

Have you ever been to a _____? Perhaps you went to a

_____ and Bailey Circus. P.T. Barnum, the father of that circus,

was the first great showman in _____. He was the first to use

_____ in show business. He also loved to fool the people.

Phineas Taylor Barnum came to _____ York in 1834 to make his

_____. He tried all kinds of tricks to bring the people to see his shows.

_____ once hired a band to _____ all day

outside his show building. The _____ was so bad, it drove the

_____ inside the building. They wanted to _____

away from the noise.

Barnum _____ not care what people said about

_____. He just wanted them to say _____ about him.

Not all Barnum's shows were tricks. He discovered Tom Thumb, a tiny man, and put

him in his show. He also presented Jenny Lind, a great singer of that time. Finally, he

began "the greatest show on earth"—the Barnum and Bailey Circus.

Name _____

A Great Showman

1. Who was P.T. Barnum?

   _____

   _____

2. What was he the first to do in show business?

   _____

   _____

3. What did he love to do to the people?

   _____

   _____

4. What trick did he play when he hired the band to play outside his show buildings?

   _____

   _____

5. What famous people did Barnum put in his show?

   _____

6. What was the name of his circus?

   _____

A Most Unusual Bet

common	games	in	the
back	he	his	He
Cole	races	noon	Paris
man's	bet	told	The
his	the	for	he

People often make bets. It is _____ for us to bet on baseball

_____ and football games. In some states, it is legal to bet on horse

_____. This, though, is a story of a most unusual bet. See if you can

guess what the bet was.

At _____, in the year 1910, on a beautiful spring day in

_____, a truck broke down. _____ driver

got out. He went under _____ truck. He came out from under

_____ truck a half hour later. He _____ the

police he was very sorry _____ the traffic jam he caused. Then

_____ drove away.

Can you guess what the _____ was? Here is the answer: The

_____ name was Horace De Vere _____, England's

greatest practical joker of the day. _____ collected several thousand

English pounds (a pound is worth about $1.50 now) from _____ friends.

He had bet that _____ could lie on his _____ for 30

minutes at _____ traffic center _____ Paris.

A Most Unusual Bet

1. List some things people bet on.

   _____

   _____

2. At what time did this incident take place?

   _____

3. Where did the incident take place?

   _____

   _____

4. What was the bet?

   _____

   _____

5. What was the practical joker's name?

   _____

6. Where did he live?

   _____

7. What is English money called?

   _____

8. How much is it worth in dollars today?

   _____

DO SNAKES FLY????
Cloze:
is, the, the, ground, holds, snake, say, of
Comprehension:
1. India
2. straight
3. in emergencies
4. No, they glide.
5. Answers will vary.

DEEP FREEZE
Cloze:
climates, 90, temperature, as, standing, freeze, it, because
Comprehension:
1. 90 degrees below zero
2. It becomes hard as stone; hard as salt.
3. You would freeze like a rock.
4. Answers will vary.
5. Answers will vary.

LARGEST LIVING ANIMAL
Cloze:
living, grown, as, much, is, throat, 9, be
Comprehension:
1. the blue whale
2. as much as 120 pickup trucks
3. elephant
4. 9 or 10 inches
5. throat too small
6. Answers will vary.

A STRANGE SHAVE
Cloze:
tall, large, the, seed, as, man, face, clean
Comprehension:
1. pulls out a stalk
2. a sharp seed
3. He might cut himself.
4. Answers will vary.
5. Answers will vary.

LAZIEST ANIMAL
Cloze:
for, hours, even, a, it, in, sags, never, even, of
Comprehension:
1. the sloth
2. It stays in the same position.
3. It doesn't bother to stand up; does nothing for hours. Will vary.
4. Answers will vary.

DOGGIE DIETS
Cloze:
dogs, up, your, sure, back, fresh, dog, progress, puppies, problems
Comprehension:
1. We feed our dogs too much.
2. one time a week
3. fresh water
4. Answers will vary.

ROWING ACROSS THE OCEAN
Cloze:
Frank, believed, to, build, could, would, the, stove, had, Sometimes, would, a, food, began
Comprehension:
1. cross the ocean in a rowboat; row to France
2. Yes, the story said they were sailors.
3. New York; France

THRILLER
Cloze:
to, really, has, hair, muscles, angry, on, not, only, of, behind, eyes, grinning, end
Comprehension:
1. Your hair can stand on end.
2. muscle
3. cat
4. Answers will vary.

HELICOPTERS
Cloze:
Almost, France, like, could, people, they, 100, that, War, be, due, used, use, owe, in
Comprehension:
1. whirlybird, egg beater, chopper
2. Chinese toy top

GOOD LUCK SPOTS
Cloze:
on, causes, luck, of, nail, the/these, make, grows, these/the, or, near, being, to, signs, tell
Comprehension:
1. imperfect growth of the nail, bruises
2. good luck spots
3. living cells

WANTED: DEAD OR ALIVE
Cloze:
"wanted", what, of, from, They, toads, the, garbage/cattle, cattle/garbage, their, reward, or, up, Jesse, seen
Comprehension:
1. Australia
2. South America
3. garbage, ping pong balls, dogs, cats, cattle, Answers will vary.

SALTIEST LAKE
Cloze:
the, It, the, is, really, water, hard/difficult, is, rocks, the, to, a, in, of, covered, difficult/hard
Comprehension:
1. Dead Sea
2. covered with oily film

MISS PIGGY
Cloze:
Pigs, I'll, of, in, instrument, pigtail, instrument, pig, pitch, were, tails, worked, To, the out, Miss, Kermit, the
Comprehension:
1. pigtail organ

DID COLUMBUS EAT ICE CREAM?
Cloze:
ice, say, even, an, she, cream, ice, 400, book, a, same, ball, that, House, of, Maryland, a
Comprehension:
1. Italy
2. 1769
3. at a ball
4. President's wife
5. 1851
6. no
7. Maryland
8. Answers will vary.

GREAT ESCAPE ARTIST
Cloze:
who, handcuffs, course, made, helper's, for, was, all, famous, in, with, pairs, Then, was, around, put, in
Comprehension:
1. Jim Collins
2. a mechanic
3. in a river
4. 5
5. put keys into the box
6. almost 20 years
7. handcuffs, box, rope, river

CLOSE ENCOUNTERS
Cloze:
visiting, seen, One, businessman, state, caught, nine, seemed, phoned, soon, that, in, to, planes, of, getting, last, were, time, from
Comprehension:
1. light; bright objects
2. called the newspaper
3. three
4. Answers will vary.
5. unidentified flying object
6. Answers will vary.

VAMPIRES LIVE
Cloze:
movie, These, 250, the, of, carry, to, birds, their, the, at, nests, off, their, Sometimes, picks, you, when, America
Comprehension:
1. in the tropics
2. suck their blood
3. rabies
4. hang them in trees or take them along
5. animals
6. bats
7. at night
8. 250

GHOST TOWNS
Cloze:
towns, there, sprang, and, ran, famous, great, 1859, 11,000, People, furniture, on, Virginia, was
Comprehension:
1. towns that have no people
2. The mines ran out.
3. Virginia City
4. silver
5. people left
6. Mark Twain

A GREAT SHOWMAN
Cloze:
circus, Barnum, America, Advertising, New, fortune, He, play, music, people, get, did, him, something
Comprehension:
1. a famous showman
2. advertise
3. fool them
4. He had the band play so badly the   people would go inside to escape   the noise.
5. Tom Thumb, Jenny Lind
6. Barnum and Bailey Circus

UNUSUAL BET
Cloze:
common, games, races, noon, Paris, The, his/the, the/his, told, for, he, bet, man's, Cole, He, his, he, back, the, in
Comprehension:
1. sports events, horses, cards; Answers will vary.
2. noon
3. Paris
4. De Vere Cole could lie on his back   in the middle of traffic in the street   for one-half hour
5. Horace De Vere Cole
6. England
7. pounds
8. $1.50 more or less